CAMEO CUTTING

BY

John B. Marsh

AUTHOR OF
"THE REFERENCE SHAKESPEARE," "VENICE AND THE VENETIANS,"
ETC.

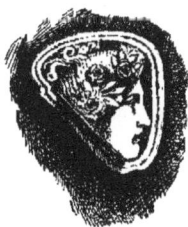

With Original Illustrations.

.

A History of Jewellery
and Jewellery Making

'Jewellery' refers to small decorative items, worn for personal adornment such as brooches, rings, necklaces, earrings and bracelets. It may be attached to any part of the body or the clothes, but the term is generally restricted to durable ornaments, excluding flowers for example. For many centuries metal, often combined with gemstones has been the normal material for jewellery, but other materials such as shells and other plant materials may be used. The oldest known piece of jewellery is actually formed from 100,000 year old beads from Nassarius (whelk) shells. The word *jewellery* itself is derived from the word *jewel*, which was anglicized from the Old French *'jouel'*, and beyond that, to the Latin word *'jocale'*, meaning plaything.

Alloys of nearly every metal known have been encountered in jewellery. Bronze, for example, was common in Roman times. Modern fine jewellery usually includes gold (measured in karats), white gold, platinum, palladium, titanium or silver. But perhaps one of the most influential jewels has been the diamond – first mined in India, it is now sourced in Australia, Botswana, Russia and Canada. Most famously, the British crown jewels contain the 'Cullinan Diamond', part of the largest gem-quality rough diamond ever found (found in 1905 at 3,106.75 carats). It is now hugely popular in engagement rings, with this use dating back to the marriage of Maximilian I to Mary of Burgundy in 1477. Other precious and semiprecious stones used for jewellery include (but are by no means limited to) amber, emerald, jade, jasper, ruby, sapphire and quartz.

In most cultures, jewellery can be understood as a status symbol – a simply beautiful object to behold, a functional (i.e. useful in the form of hair pins, or for spiritual protection in the form of amulets), or a culturally important signifier of meaning. Many peoples, in all periods of history have kept large amounts of wealth stored in the form of jewellery. Numerous cultures move wedding dowries in the form of jewellery, and use these same items as currencies or trade goods; an example being the use of 'slave beads' (literally used to barter for people). Jewellery can also be symbolic of group membership, as in the case of the Christian crucifix or the Jewish Star of David. In creating these pieces incredibly precious materials are often used such as gemstones, rare metals and especially gold.

As already evidenced, jewellery itself has a massively long history and the first signs of its usage came from the peoples of Africa. Perforated beads suggesting shell jewellery made from sea snail shells have been found dating to 75,000 years ago at Blombos Cave (just east of Cape Town). Outside of Africa, the Cro-Magnons (early Europeans) had crude necklaces and bracelets of bone, teeth, berries and stones, strung on pieces of string or animal sinew. The Venus of Hohle Fels (Germany) features a perforation at the top, showing that it was intended to be worn as a pendant. Some of the most prolific jewellery wearers were the Egyptians however, and around 3,000 years ago the first signs of established jewellery making were found in Egypt.

The Egyptians (like we do today) preferred the luxury, rarity and workability of gold over other metals. It soon began to symbolise power and especially religious power within the community - worn by the wealthiest citizens in life, as well as death. In conjunction with gold jewellery, Egyptians used coloured glass, along with precious gems – the colours holding great significance. Green, for example, symbolised fertility. The Greeks also started using gold and gems in jewellery around 1600 BC, although beads shaped as shells and animals were produced widely in earlier times. Beadwork was in fact one of the most popular and widely available forms of jewellery. By 300 BC, the Greeks had mastered making coloured jewellery using amethysts, pearl and emeralds. Greek jewellery was often simpler than other cultures, with streamlined designs and workmanship; mostly used for public appearances or on special occasions. It was most frequently given as a gift, mostly to women and was especially revered for its protection from the 'Evil Eye' or endowing the owner with supernatural or religious significance.

As we move closer to the present day, the Renaissance signalled a massive change in European jewellery production. Exploration and new sciences led to increased availability of gemstones, as well as exposure to the art of other cultures. Whereas prior to this, the working of gold and precious metal had been at the forefront of Jewellery, this period saw increasing dominance of gemstones and their settings. The early

Victorian period featured many nature-inspired designs, often with intricate etchings in gold settings; lockets and brooches were popular daytime wear, whereas coloured gemstones and diamonds were de-rigueur in the evening. Because the later, 'Grand Victorian' period corresponded with the death of Queen Victoria's husband, many later pieces had solemn, sombre designs, featuring heavy, dark stones such as jet, onyx an d amethyst. These subdued designs quickly disappeared as we move towards the 1900s however – where bright gemstones and feminine designs were all the rage.

In the Twentieth Century, following the First World War, Art Deco styles became popular – forms which utilised simpler designs and more effective manufacturing techniques. Walter Gropius and the German Bauhaus movement, with their philosophy of 'no barriers between artists and craftsmen' also led to some interesting and stylistically simplified jewellery designs. Modern materials were also introduced: plastics and aluminium were first used in jewellery, and of note are the chromed pendants of Russian-born Bauhaus master Naum Slutzky. Today, artisan jewellery continues to grow both as a hobby and profession, with periodicals, guilds, groups and communities embracing modern jewellery creation, as well as the values of traditional workmanship.

Nowhere have the skills of the traditional jewellery worker been more pertinent than in jewellery repair and for most businesses today, repairs tend to be one of the largest sources of income. It is such an integral part of the modern jewellery industry that the average bench jeweller is likely to have taken at least one professional course in jewellery restoration. The fact that repairs, alongside jewellery creation, have come to form such an integral part of the industry highlight the enduring importance of jewellery to civilisations all over the globe. Jewellery has been used for its functionality, beauty and value since prehistoric times and continues to be used for exactly the same purposes today. Whilst the items themselves have changed, their significance to us has not. We hope the reader enjoys this book.

1890

A PRIMROSE SHELL,
By Signor Giovanni.

INTRODUCTION.

THE art of cutting Cameos in shell is of so very
recent birth, compared with that of working in
precious stones, that a claim to consideration in
setting forth the method and practice may justly
be preferred. Yet my little treatise, which is
based upon practical experience, has been found,
even in more limited form, a sufficient guide for
the practice of the art, by a large number of
amateurs in England, Wales, and Switzerland, to
produce good work; these were all of them skilled
in the use of the brush, the pencil, or the chisel.
To all similarly proficient in any department of
art, Cameo-cutting will be found a pleasant and
interesting employment.

CONTENTS.

———◆———

	PAGE
SHELL CAMEO-CUTTING	11
SHELL CAMEOS IN THE MUSEUMS	19
APPEARANCE OF THE CONCH-SHELL	19
ADAPTABILITY OF THE ART	22
COST OF PIECES OF SHELL	25
CARVED PUMICE-STONE	26
MOUNTING PIECES OF SHELL	26
DRAWING THE DESIGN	29
THE TOOLS	30
THE USE OF THE HOLDFAST	32
PROCESS OF WORKING	34
WORKING BY NIGHT	41
POLISHING	41
SHARPENING THE TOOLS	42
COST OF APPLIANCES	43
DECLINE IN THE FASHION OF WEARING CAMEOS .	44
CAMEO-CUTTING HIGHLY RECOMMENDED . . .	47
DERIVATION OF THE WORD "CAMEO" . . .	51
A TEACHER AT WORK	55
LESSONS BY CORRESPONDENCE	57
IS THERE A MARKET?	58
DESIGNS	60

HANDBOOK

CAMEO-CUTTING.

——◆——

Shell Cameo-Cutting.

THE discovery of the adaptation of the Conch-
shell to the art of the Cameo engraver is traceable
no farther back than the beginning of the reign
of Her Gracious Majesty the Queen. The working of Cameos in precious stones, however, goes
back beyond the earliest historical records ; history
contains no reference to the beginning or progress
of the development. Tradition declares that the
art was of Asiatic origin, and that it was practised by the Babylonians, from whom the Phœni-
cians carried it into Egypt. Thence the progress
of the work is clearly traced to Greece and Italy,
and in our own time to France and England.
Those who have practised Cameo engraving in
England may be numbered on the fingers of one
hand. But it is not with the carving of precious
stones this handbook deals, but with the youngest

of all the processes discovered in connection with the production of the Cameo, that of working the beautiful Conch-shell.

The use of this shell for the purpose of Cameo-cutting was first practised in Italy, about the year 1820, and it was then believed to be of Sicilian origin. For many years all the shells used were exported from England, and the number averaged about three hundred per annum; these were valued at 30s. each. They soon became a favourite medium in Rome with the workmen, and the art was taken thence to Paris, where it flourished. In 1847 the sale of shells was reported to have reached 100,500, and their declared value was £8900, while the Cameos which were produced were estimated to be worth at least £40,000.

The prices of shells have since been very much reduced owing to an increased importation, so that shells of great beauty may now be purchased for 10s.; while they may be had in quantities as low as 1s. 6d. each. Choice black shells, however, still command a higher price.

The colour of the ground in these shells varies from pink and orange to an absolute black: this is called the Black Helmet (*Cassis Tuberosa*), and comes from the West Indian Seas. The shell with a pink ground is called the Queen Conch (*Strombus Gigas*), and is also brought from the West Indies. A favourite variety is the Bull's Mouth (*Cassis Rufa*), found in the East Indian

Seas, which has a sard-like ground. Another class is the Horned Helmet (*Cassis Cornuta*), which is brought from Madagascar; in this the ground is dark claret in colour. Occasionally shells are made use of having three layers, the upper, always dark-coloured, serving for the hair, or a wreath, or for armour; the second layer, which is always white, is used for carving the figure; and the third layer is the ground.

Messrs. Francati & Santamaria,[1] of Hatton Garden, were the largest and almost the only dealers in shells for Cameo work in the Metropolis, and they cut them up to the exact size required for engraving. I have seen in their cellars many thousands of Conch-shells brought from foreign seas for the purpose of being cut up for export to Italy or Paris. Mr. Santamaria, upon one occasion, showed me a magnificent Black Helmet shell, which he said was the only one that had been discovered out of about ten thousand. A shell of ordinary size only produces, on being cut up, three or four large workable pieces, and these are worth from 3s. to 5s. each; but the Bull Mouth, of small size, may be purchased for a shilling. A face or figure engraved upon a shell looks well, particularly when the taste of the artist enables him to cover every knob with figures, and form an appropriate border

---

[1] Partnership now dissolved.

of leaves round the whole ; even the circles round the apex of the shell lend themselves to ornamentation, and shells carved all over are much sought after. An experienced workman will often employ his leisure in covering a large shell with work in this way. In the centre he places the principal design, always a classic figure or group of figures, and around, such ornamentation as his taste approves. One of these, cut in Hatton Garden, was sold recently for a hundred guineas ; and another, almost entirely cut by Mr. W. King, a young Englishman then in the employment of Messrs. Francati & Santamaria, sold for £80.

The most celebrated Cameo engraver of modern times was Benedetto Pistrucci, who designed the "George and Dragon" of our coinage, which is acknowledged to be the finest work that has ever appeared in modern currency. Of himself he says that he was in a manner born to the work he took up from choice, and he mentions in proof of this that he had square thumbs, and the palm of his right hand was covered with horny skin. This had been a characteristic with certain of the males in the family for several generations. He was the son of a judge, and was born at Rome in May 1784. His eldest brother was a painter, and every member of the family was endowed with artistic tastes. Italy, in his youth, was overrun by the French, which caused his parents to make frequent changes of residence. At fourteen years of age, being then proficient in drawing, he was first put to a master, one Signor Mango, who, perceiving his genius, employed him to make designs for his Cameos. This provoked much jealousy among the other workmen, one of whom stabbed Benedetto with a dagger. During his illness he amused himself by modelling the figures he drew, and so perfected himself in the stages necessary for becoming a thorough artist; less than this in training will only make a workman. Upon his recovery he was sent to two masters in succession, the second of whom, noticing the superiority of his designs, exclaimed, "With one who has genius there is very little for a master to teach." At sixteen years of age he began work on his own account; and, after a brief courtship, at eighteen years of age, married a girl of sixteen, of gentle family. There were born to them two daughters, Victoria and Eliza, and one son, Vincenzio. Eliza and her brother were endowed with the paternal characteristic, a horny palm, and became celebrated as workers in Cameo. At twenty-four years of age Benedetto had succeeded in establishing a reputation as an engraver of precious stones, having taught himself the process, and constructed with his own hands the wheel with which he worked. For several years he had sold Cameos worked in stones to one Angelo Bonelli, a travelling dealer in gems; and discovering one day that a specimen of his work had been stained to represent an antique, and sold for a high price, he resolved for the future to place a secret mark upon those he sold. On one of these, the head of Flora, he cut two Greek letters in the hair. The condition of Italy at that time induced him to consider the advantage of proceeding to England; but before emigrating he executed several orders for one of Napoleon's sisters, one portrait being cut in stone, much smaller than a fly. Pistrucci brought to London a letter of introduction to Mr. Konig, mineralogist of the British Museum, and by Lord Fife he was introduced to Sir Joseph Banks. The latter afterwards introduced him to Mr. Payne Knight, who produced at their interview what he called the finest Greek Cameo in existence, a most choice gem, a fragment of the head of Flora, for which he had paid Bonelli 5co guineas. Pistrucci did not even take the stone from the extended palm of Mr. Knight; a glance disclosed the fact that it was that head of Flora in whose hair he had cut two Greek letters, and for which Bonelli had paid him £5. An unpleasant scene resulted. The letters were plainly visible; but Bonelli, realising that his trade was at an end, boldly denounced Pistrucci. He pointed to the wreath of flowers about the head in proof of his conceit that it was an antique, asserting that no such flowers were then in existence; but Sir Joseph Banks, examining them with a microscope, ex-

claimed, "The flowers are roses, as I am a
botanist!" Pistrucci offered to carve another
Flora exactly similar without looking again at
the "antique." This challenge was not accepted.
Then it was agreed that he should cut a head of
Flora in a different position, and this was accepted
as a test of the truth of his representations. The
story soon spread through London society; noble-
men, scientific men, ladies of rank, watched the
growth of the new Flora under the hands of
Pistrucci, and when it was completed the dispute
raged with increased bitterness, so that Payne
Knight's antique Flora became the question of
the day. The controversy at length ended with
universal expressions of sympathy for Mr. Payne
Knight.*

This stone may be seen in the Gold Ornament
Room at the British Museum. It is placed in
the case of "Modern Engraved Gems," upon
which stands the Alabaster vase engraved with
the name of Xerxes, and is in the bottom row
of the case. The face is exquisitely beautiful,
and the roses which are cut in the upper
coloured layer of the stone are perfect. An
attendant will point out this Flora to any one
who asks for it.

Pistrucci upon one occasion, while still residing
in Rome, had an antique pale-brown sard given
him to recut by Domenico Desalief. The subject

---

[1] See title-page.

was a warrior crowned by a female, but so clumsily executed as to be of little value. There was, however, plenty of material to cut away. After taking an impression in wax, he altered the whole; then he cut away the knees of the figures, and recut them higher up, and so remodelled the design that not a trace was left of the original forms. The dealer was delighted, and sold the gem readily for the Imperial Russian Cabinet of St. Petersburg, where it still remains, and is regarded as of the highest value.

The dispute about the Flora indirectly brought about Pistrucci's appointment to the Mint as chief engraver, and he designed and executed the "George and Dragon" among other works. Afterwards a considerable amount of jealousy was created by his employment amongst the officers of the Mint, and the members of the Royal Academy were divided about his appointment, one portion insisting that native talent should be encouraged, the other division holding that he was the best living engraver. To restore peace, his appointment was subsequently styled that of "chief medallist." He cut two portraits of Her Majesty in onyx, one as Princess, and the other as Queen wearing a diadem. On retiring from the Mint he took a cottage at Old Windsor, where he died in his seventy-first year, in 1855, only thirty-five years ago, and recently enough for him to be well remembered by a few living men. His connection with our own day, and the distinction to which one of his pupils has risen, justify the introduction of his name into this book. His daughters, before their father's death, returned to Rome, where they practised Cameo-cutting with great success.

Shell Cameos in the Museums.

There are in the collections shown in the Mediæval Room of the British Museum several fine specimens of shell Cameos which date from mediæval times, but these shells were found in the Mediterranean; and at South Kensington there are a few specimens of shell Cameos worked in Rome. The only illustrations of the art of progressive working in the Conch-shell in any museum in London are to be seen in the South Court of South Kensington, where the portrait of Millais is shown in the several stages of progress, together with the shell from which the piece worked was originally cut. These interesting specimens were presented by Mr. James Ronca, who was a pupil of Pistrucci's brother. There are, of course, many separate specimens of carved Conch-shells, in whole and in pieces, at both the British and South Kensington Museums.

Appearance of the Conch-shell.

The shell will be readily recognised without an illustration. In form somewhat resembling the human ear, the shell possesses properties which can be found in no other specimen of the order. For the purposes of the engraver, the several parts are called by totally different names, according as the workman came from Naples or Rome; but without entering into a discussion of the origin of these, I propose to give a few plain names to the several parts, in order to enable a worker to order the particular piece or portion which is required. Thus, the several parts are the back of the shell, the back of the Lip, the Dome, and the Comb, the Mouth of the shell, the Lip, and the Face or Body.

The piece in the upper portion of the Dome is the most valuable, because in that there is no variation of colour. Pieces cut from all other portions of the shell vary slightly in depth of colour, the colour deepening in tone as the mouth is approached. A piece suitable for a brooch cut out of a Black Helmet would be worth 5s.; but with regard to other shells the prices vary as set out in the following list. Other portions of the Dome are used for brooches; but the choicest piece is the one named. The Comb, having been cut off, is cut up into separate knobs, and these are worked into heads which are required to stand out in bold relief. The back edge is rarely worked, and may be regarded as waste. The Lip is the next important portion, and this is suitable for the carved handles of paper-knives, for umbrella-handles, or for paper-weights. A full length figure of classic form may be carved in the Lip, with admirable results, so as to command a high price. The Lip is perhaps more frequently cut into pieces between the raised edges which run at right angles to the course of the mouth, and are used for carving fish or birds, or any form requiring a portion in high relief. When the Dome has been cut through, a second shell appears immediately below, and this is remarkable for having three distinct layers, brown or red forming the surface, white the centre, and brown or red the ground. Such a piece is necessary where the design involves ornaments in the hair or a helmet on the head of a warrior.

The shell is cut open by means of a tin wheel revolving on a spindle in the ordinary way by means of a treadle. Above the wheel is a sloping dish coming to a point on which emery powder lies, and above the tray is a small keg of water regulated by a stop-cock, in such a way that as the water trickles down the pan it carries particles of the powder on to the wheel. The workman first cuts off the Lip, then he cuts across, above and below the Comb, and finally cuts down from the point of the Dome to the Comb again. This triangular piece is cut up into as many portions as are required, care being taken first of all to cut out the choicest piece from the upper portion.

Adaptability of the Art.

The practice of the art of Cameo-cutting solves to a certain extent one aspect of the great problem now puzzling the most astute minds—how to find remunerative work for skilled hands. Here is a field at present quite unoccupied—an industry admirably adapted to thousands already trained in the requirements of art, and only needing the suggestion to enable them to realise the fruit of years of industrious and patient study. In this, as in all other artistic occupations, there must be a groundwork on which to ensure success. Any one ignorant alike of the principles of drawing or modelling or carving can never become proficient in the art of Cameo-cutting, though by patient labour success may be obtained as a copyist, and the worker be able to cut geometric patterns, flowers, and coats-of-arms, which would command a ready market. For the higher successes attainable by a Cameo engraver, the position of a true artist, whose work would be recognised by the form of a hand or the modelling of an eye or an ear, there must be a previous knowledge of drawing, with skill in modelling and ability to carve.

Nothing less than a first place should content the Cameo-worker. The age is one which is eminently suitable for the growth of the profession. Drawing has for many years been taught in Schools of Art on scientific principles, and pupils have proceeded from drawing to modelling, to carving in wood, or to painting in water and oils in these schools, until a point of excellence has been reached thought impossible before they were established. Even in the rate-sustained Board Schools children of tender years are taught to draw with surprising accuracy, and such of them as take pleasure in their work might very easily learn how to cut simple forms suitable for buttons or bracelets. The only thing they would have to acquire would be the use of the graver, following upon the work of the pencil. Nor is this an exaggeration, because two little girls of eight and ten, from watching their father at work, actually fashioned little vases and hearts in pieces of shell by using fine files. From children as inexperienced as these, and from such an elementary knowledge of drawing as the School Board imparts to the young, up to the most experienced artist,—the gold medallist, the born genius with pencil or chisel,—there is enough in Cameo-work to supply scope for all—enough to gratify the child's wish, and the larger ambition ; and, beyond the choicest specimen of art in existence, enough to leave still greater triumphs to be realised by future workers. By the practice of this art no industry at present in existence in England would be injured ; but, on the contrary, many industries, such as those of the workers in silver and gold, the wood-carver, and the cabinet-maker, would receive fresh development. The present generation has never been in a position to consider this industry as one attainable by the people until the present time; nor would the Cameo supplant any artistic article at present enjoying public favour. Cameos may be carved small enough to adorn a lady's ring, a gentleman's shirt-stud, or a pin. They may be mounted for bracelets, or act as pendants, or brooches, or be used for hairpins, for buttons to fasten back the vest, or for jackets; as solitaires for the shirt, or for sleeve-links. In the style of ladies' dress now worn there would be an unfailing demand. They may be fixed in articles of ornament for the desk and table, inlaid in vases, caskets, or dressing-cases; framed in the carved overmantel, inserted in the backs of chairs, inset in curtain bands; or mounted on altar crosses, set around Communion-cups or in alms-dishes, or worked into marble memorials of the dead; or they might be inlet in the bindings of books. From the variety of their ground—ranging from pink, through every shade of brown, to an imperial purple, and a magnificent black—there is no marble, metal, or wood with which the Cameo would not harmonise. In the course of a conversation recently with one of our Princesses, who is a patron of art, this point was dwelt upon, and the suggestion was made that an anchor carved in shell would make an appropriate button for a lady's yachting costume.

Cost of Pieces of Shell.

The cost of ordinary pieces of shell per dozen may be ascertained by reference to the following diagrams :—

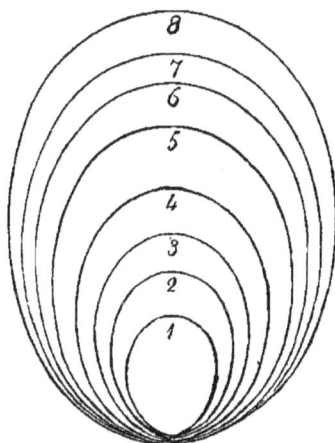

Fig. 1.—Different Sizes of Pieces.

Nos. 1 and 2, suitable for small and large earrings, 3s. per dozen; No. 3, bracelet size, 4s.; No. 4, larger bracelet or small brooch, 6s.; No. 5, large brooch, 8s.; No. 6, 10s.; No. 7, 15s. to 18s., according to the colour; No. 8, 2s. 6d. to 3s. 6d. each.

The importers of these shells would make up a dozen of various sizes if required. Great care is necessary in selecting pieces suitable for working in order to avoid (1) the mark of a worm left in the early growth of the shell; (2) patches of decayed shell; (3) a tendency to chip, termed " flaking."

Carved Pumice-stone.

An experienced Cameo engraver recommends a beginner to procure pieces of Pumice-stone, which may be readily obtained, and begin by carving in this substance. The stone is much softer than the shell, and can be very easily shaped; and the colour lends itself to very beautiful effects, but the surface being very soft, the fine work soon disappears. As an intermediate step to the carving on the Conch-shell, the Pumice-stone may be strongly recommended.

Mounting Pieces of Shell.

When it has been determined to carve a piece of shell, the first thing to be done is to mount it upon what is technically known as a Stick. Get the handle of a broom, cut off five inches, and cover each end with cement made of a mixture of tar and resin. This may be procured at any oil-shop. Ask for a cake of cement, and you get a square for a 1d. which would suffice for twenty or thirty pieces of shell, or you may buy a pound for 6d. or 8d. Melt the cement as you would a piece of sealing-wax, cover each end of the Stick with the melted stuff, so as to form a bed; wet the under part of the shell, and press it into the cement. This will hold the piece firmly while it is being worked. By mounting a piece of shell on each end of the Stick, there is the advantage of working upon two patterns at the same time, or of cutting the same pattern twice, improving upon one by the experience obtained in cutting the other.

In selecting an oval piece for working, care should be taken to get one without flaw. This is a difficult matter, and requires a great deal of experience. Beginners should select pieces tolerably smooth; but practised workers prefer those which are irregular in their surface, because they furnish more scope for the exercise of their skill. In cutting these, the design follows the convolution of the shell. It is dangerous to lower any one portion, because the white surface does not preserve the same relative thickness all over the piece; and unless care is taken the ground will show through. This is not a disadvantage in the ear or the neck, but would be serious if it was apparent on the forehead or in the cheek. A skilful Cameo-cutter will, however, so arrange his design as to produce the blush of the ground in such portions as to enhance the value of his work. In drawing the face, avoid, if possible, the rough, rotten-looking patches. These are signs of decay which may only be superficial, and disappear at the first cut; but, on the contrary, they are more likely to penetrate deeply, and may necessitate the lowering of the whole face before they can be got rid of altogether.

Sometimes, when the face has been modelled, and nothing remains but the finishing, a crooked line appears, which Cameo-cutters believe is caused by the presence of a worm in the early development of the shell. This is very difficult to get rid of; hence extreme care is necessary in selecting the piece for working.

A third fault is "flaking," when, by a single cut, the whole of the forehead chips off, or half the nose disappears. There is no remedy then; the whole face must be cut in low relief, or the piece be thrown aside altogether; the latter is often the more preferable course. But all these risks are minimised by experience. Having got a satisfactory piece mounted, the Stick is held in the left hand, and the face drawn upon it in lead-pencil, a little larger than the size actually required.

If a whole shell is to be carved, care must be taken in the first instance to cleanse it. To do this, get a small quantity of muriatic acid and wash with a brush; this will bring away all the dirt; then add to some fresh muriatic acid hot water, immerse the shell for one or two minutes; then rinse the shell in cold water.

Holtzaffpel, referring to the outlining of the

design, recommends that every portion be left rather in excess, so that there may be ample room for improving the outline in finishing off. Be very careful not to injure the ground, as the natural surface is superior to any that can be given artificially.

Drawing the Design.

Beginners should draw the design or figure first upon a piece of paper, or model it in clay or wax, and then draw the pattern upon the shell.

FIG. 2.—Transferring Head to Shell.

If the surface of the shell is irregular, do not attempt to make it level, but follow the irregularities, remembering that the white stratum is of the same thickness all through the piece, and that if the surface is filed down the ground will show through, disfiguring the appearance of the design, and preventing the pattern being modelled in proper proportions. When the design is settled

upon, copy it on the shell with the help, if necessary, of a star, as in the head (Fig. 2).   Draw the
outline slightly larger than the design, so as to
allow of the proper proportions being secured on
cutting.   Skilful Cameo engravers never use a
pencil, but sketch the desired outline with one or
other of the cutting-tools; and many of them
could not draw the figure on a piece of paper
which they readily cut with their tools.

The Tools.

There are at present none specially made for
the use of the Cameo engraver in England, but
all that are required may be selected from those
kept in stock for the use of engravers.

Mr. G. Buck, 242 Tottenham Court Road,
London, W., keeps the tools most suitable for
Cameo-work separate, and can supply them on
request.   They are of two kinds, round and flat
Scawpers and Spit-stickers, and cost, handled,
3d. each.   To these may be added a Fine File, and
the stock is complete, exhibiting in this respect
a striking contrast to the price of tools necessary
for practising many other useful arts.   The Round
Scawpers are used for first cutting the figure and
developing the several parts, the Flat Scawpers
for smoothing the work, and the Spit-sticker for
putting in the finishing touches.

The following diagrams show the exact size of the several tools :—

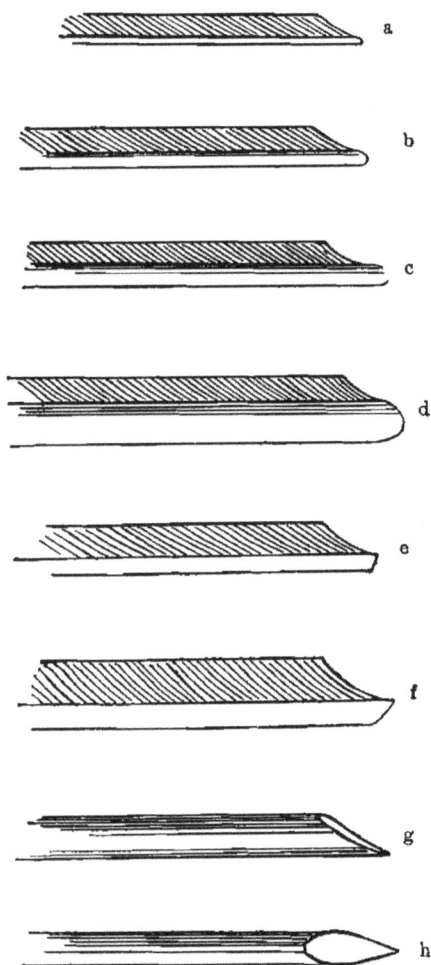

Figs. a to h, Tools for Cameo-work.

The following diagrams show the Flat and

Round Scawper, handled, and sections of each (Figs. 4 and 4a, 5 and 5a).

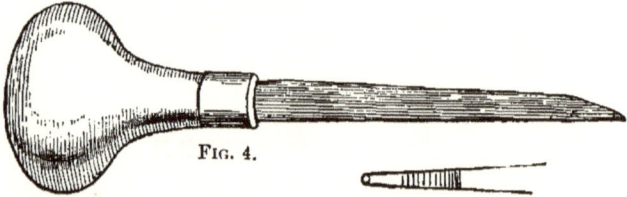

FIG. 4.

FIG. 4a.

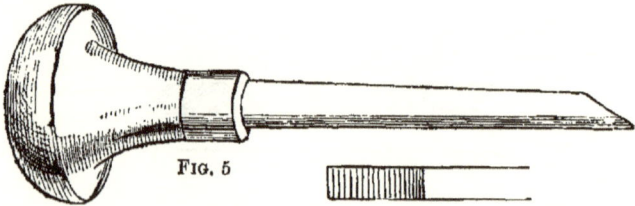

FIG. 5

FIG. 5a.

Handled Tools and Sections of them.

The Use of the Holdfast.

The piece of shell having been mounted on a Stick, a grip is wanted in which to hold the Stick with the left hand, while work is carried on with the right hand. This may be obtained by using a piece of wood, like that in the illustration (Fig. 6), and screwing it to the top of a wooden table, so that the notch is projected a couple of inches in advance of the edge of the table; or, if no special table is available, a Holdfast should be purchased, such as is shown in Fig. 6. This is screwed to the edge of a table from below, and fits any kind of table, leaving no mark whatever. The price of a Holdfast varies from 1s. to 2s. 6d., and the article may be purchased at any tool-

Fig. 6.—Holdfast.

shop. A simpler form of Holdfast may be obtained by purchasing an iron screw-clip, which may be had from any ironmonger, and getting a notched piece of wood, as shown in the above cut, and this is considered preferable by many as furnishing a steadier grip while work is going on.

C

Process of Working.

Whatever may be the figure or pattern to be
cut, the process is the same with respect to the
handling of the tools. The wooden handle lies in
the palm of the right hand, and all the power is
imparted by the palm. As the material operated
upon is almost as hard as marble, power is required to make a cut; but if the tools are well-tem-
pered and very sharp, a little experience will soon
teach the cutter how to work. The thumb of the
right hand should be protected by a finger-stall
from injury by the edge of the tool. In the illustration (Fig. 7) the method of holding the stick

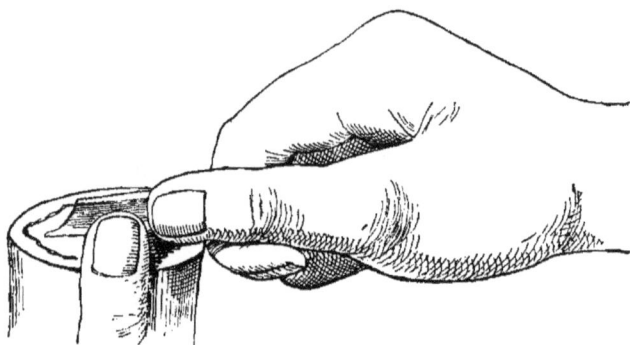

FIG. 7.

is shown in conjunction with the method of holding the tool. The thumb of the left hand rises
the height of the nail above the top of the Stick;
against this the thumb of the right hand is placed,
which furnishes the necessary resistance to the

power created by the palm of the right hand; the finger and thumb then direct the cut which is to be made by the Scawper.

Supposing the figure drawn to be a face, cut outline with tool Fig. A; block out and model features roughly with D; form ornaments on head and outline hair with C; develop more clearly with A and B. The face can next be prepared with C, by one cut from brow to nose, and another from nose to chin. With B separate the hair from the forehead, outline the ear, divide the mouth and nose from the cheek by an upward cut to the eyebrow; from the corner of the nose cut a triangle—this will form the eye. Make two cuts for nostril and chin; midway between these another cut will mark the mouth; sink the neck, outline the collar and dress; the face is then "roughed." The eye, nostrils, and mouth are cut with B, and further developed with A. The hair is divided into masses with B, separated into tresses with A, the whole sharply cut with the Spit-sticker G, and finally smoothed with E and F.

When the whole face has been roughed, it is interesting to watch a Cameo engraver at work. With a Scawper in his hand, he makes cuts all over the face, indents the cheek, smooths the ear, fashions the nostrils, lowers the nose, works at the mouth, forms the lips, cuts the chin, rounds the little triangle which contains the eye, marks the arrangement of the hair with a cut here and there, trims the beard, and so passes over the whole face again and again, bringing every portion into harmony before finishing any one feature. After the triangle has been duly rounded, and the eyebrow formed, a single cut separates the two lids of the eye, and lowers the eyeball at the same moment. When the eye is open the likeness is complete; a portrait becomes apparent when the nose and mouth are cut, but the fashioning of the eye is necessary to make it perfect. The ear and hair play important parts in completing the face. To fashion the hair requires a great amount of skill, and the beginner is timid in making cuts, but is aided in forming the curved tresses by turning the Stick with the left hand to meet the Scawper used in the right hand. A fine Scawper is necessary to cut the whiskers and beard, and the cuts should be short and curved. When the whole face has been modelled to the satisfaction of the worker, the third process begins—that of Finishing. In this operation the Spit-sticker plays a very important part. The upper eyelid is under-cut, which adds very much to the appearance of the eye; the hair is also traversed by the Spit-sticker, as well as the beard, and the tool smooths while it cuts. Finally, a Flat Graver is used to smooth forehead, cheeks, nose, and chin, taking out all marks of cuts, and softening the appearance of the whole. The hand soon becomes accustomed to the use of the tools,

and the timid cut of the learner is exchanged for
the graceful and vigorous stroke of the artist.

Holtzaffpel impresses upon all Cameo engravers
the importance of cutting all the edges of the
figure quite square from the ground, and not

Fig. A.

Fig. B.

Fig. C.

gradually rounding them down to the surface.
This is effected by under-cutting the edge where
it rests upon the ground.

Let the beginner try a few floral outlines such
as shown in Figs. A, B, and C.

When sufficient progress has been made to justify attempting to cut a face, the learner should begin with separate features—the ear, the mouth, the nose, or the eye, as in the following sketches :—

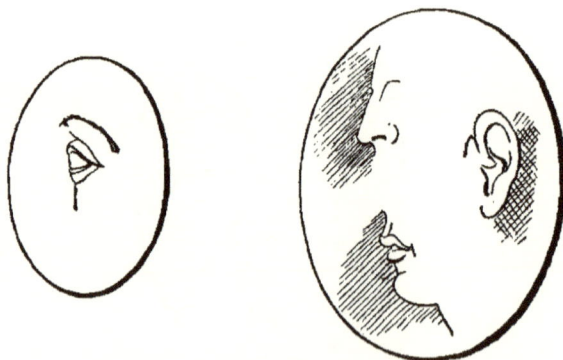

Or the features alone, as below :—

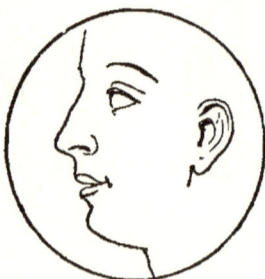

The next stage would be to form a head complete; and the following would be suitable for trial. The hair will require a considerable amount of care at first, but by perseverance all difficulties vanish; and when the features can be cut to the satisfaction of the engraver, then a whole face should be tried where no likeness is necessary.

Before attempting any portion of a face, one who is learning should first cut a few simple patterns, such as the following, which would serve as buttons for the mantle which is worn. The

tools should be used in the order given for the
several processes already mentioned.

The faces below will give an idea of the effect
produced by the process of "roughing;" and the
same face when finished off.

Roughed.

Finished.

The depth of white upon a piece of shell is insufficient to cut a face in relief, except for very small heads, which would be quite beyond the skill of a beginner. There is a beauty as well as character in the profile completely lost in the full face; yet photographers are greatly disinclined to make a *carte-de-visite* of the profile.

Working by Night.

If the work is done at night, an Engraver's glass is requisite in order to concentrate the light without glare upon the shell. There are two kinds of these glasses; one is filled with water in which sulphate of copper is dissolved, and clarified with oil of vitriol; the other, which costs 10s., consists of a large green glass eye, which moves up and down a brass rod, and is screwed to the required height. This is the better glass to use, as the oil of vitriol, however much diluted, would, by the accidental breakage of the globe, cause the destruction of any carpet over which the liquid ran. But no glass is required during the day-time, and no artificial light is equal to the natural light of day; work should therefore be confined to hours before dark.

Polishing.

When the face or figure has been finished, the ground must be cleared for polishing. Great care must be taken during the work not to cut down into the natural ground, marks being very difficult to efface. Use the Round Scawper to remove the white, and then the Flat tool to remove all traces of the white. Next cut up a bit of firewood into small lengths, point each length, and rub the surface of the Cameo with powdered pumice-stone and water, then wash with warm water and soap, with the aid of a nail-brush. With a fresh piece of wood, rub the ground with pumice-powder and oil until the surface is perfectly smooth and without a trace of cut or mark of any kind; wash once more, then apply the final polish. Take a fresh bit of wood, and mix on a plate as much dust of Rotten-Stone as will lie on a shilling, with a few drops of Sulphuric Acid, forming a yellow paste. Rub a small portion of the ground at a time, and remove the paste while still wet; if the paste is allowed to dry, it destroys the texture of the ground. After the ground has been gone over, rinse the Cameo in cold water. To remove the shell from the Stick, cut away the cement from the edge, then hold the Stick upright against the edge of a table, and give it a smart rap with a small hammer; the Cameo will slip off the top unhurt.

Sharpening the Tools.

The Cameo-worker should always have a small oilstone at hand, and a few rapid strokes will restore the fine cutting edge of his tool, but the tool must be held the reverse way of working when applied to the oilstone. Hold the tool with the cutting edge downwards on the oilstone, at the same angle as a pen is held for writing, and move rapidly to and fro five or six times; this will restore the edge immediately.

Cost of Appliances.

Holdfast or Clip, from 6d. to 2s. 6d.; four Rounded and two Flat Scawpers, 1s. 6d.; one Spit-sticker, 3d.; one File, 3d.; Cake of Cement, 1d.; Broom-handle, 2d.; one dozen pieces of Shell, various sizes, 5s.; Oilstone, 1s. to 2s.

If the cost of the tools is compared with the expenditure necessary on many occupations to which thousands devote their talents in spare hours, it will be admitted that Cameo-cutting carries the palm for cheapness. When it is further considered that this may be resorted to for an hour at any time, and does not involve the use of any machinery for its pursuit, nor the exclusive possession of any special table; while it is absolutely free from any dirt or dust injurious to furniture, to the carpet, or to the dress; that it is not trying to the sight, and not attended with risk to the hands, it must be apparent that in Cameo-cutting an occupation is presented which has undoubted claims to consideration.

All who engage in the art become fascinated by the results which are obtained. Children of tender years quickly become absorbed in the work, which not only trains the eye and the hand, but elevates and corrects the taste. To what more pleasant use could a child put the knowledge it has gained at school ? But it is not principally as an occupation for children that Cameo-cutting should be considered. Between the simple forms which a child may cut and the classic groups, such as abound, there is scope for the exercise of every degree of talent. There are artists in Cameo now in Rome and Paris whose touches are readily identified whatever they treat, in the same way that the strokes of a famous sculptor are recognised.

Decline in the Fashion of Wearing Cameos.

There were two principal causes for the decline of fashion in the wearing of Cameos in England. The first arose from paucity of designs ; and the second from the bad workmanship engendered by overwhelming orders being thrust upon a market in which only a limited number of operatives were engaged. With regard to the first cause, modern Cameo-cutters found no other models than those which had been handed down from the times of the ancient workers in gems. The cutters were copyists merely, not true artists, and

modern taste was not satisfied with the represen-
tation of classic deities, however daintily wrought.
There was no variety in the pose of figure, and
the minutest detail was settled one or two
thousand years before. Thus Apollo, Diana,
Jupiter, Mercury, Sappho, and Venus were represented in precisely the same manner they had
been a thousand times before, and the Cameo
worn by a noble lady only differed in the quality
of execution from that worn by a greengrocer's
daughter.

How the sudden demand for Cameos arose it
is difficult to say, but orders were poured into
Paris houses, and the little colony of Italian and
French workers found themselves unexpectedly
flooded with wealth. They were men possessed
of most skilful hands, but very ignorant and
untutored economists, and they worked hard for
a portion of the week only, and too often shut
themselves up in low wine-houses, and with cards
and dominoes whiled away their time. Their
wages were soon exhausted by drink and gam-
bling; and when masters wanted workmen, they
had first to settle the scores they had run up, for
the payment of which the landlords detained
them. The natural result followed, the quality
of work deteriorated, and prices fell considerably;
then houses undersold each other, and Cameos
were cut at per dozen instead of per piece. When
the Franco-German war commenced the Cameo

trade was at its lowest point, and the outbreak of hostilities dispersed the major number of the workers.

Now that the Cameo is again coming into favour, there has been produced an imitation in some hard vitreous substance, which is constantly palmed off as the genuine article to careless purchasers. I bought two of these imitation Cameos in a jeweller's shop for a few pence one day; they were both mounted and pinned for brooches. One, which was an imitation stone Cameo, bore Raphael's angels—those lovely little figures which appear at the foot of the "Madonna and Infant Christ" now in Dresden. This measures one by one and a half inches. The other was an oval, measuring one and a half by one and three-quarter inches, bearing the head of Ceres, and was an imitation shell Cameo. In this piece the ground was coloured yellow, and in exact imitation of a real piece of shell, the colour increased in depth of shading from the face to the back of the head. The face only was white, and the ornaments about the hair, three ears of corn, five roses, five forget-me-nots, tress on the neck, and necklet of pearls were in exact imitation of the well-known face. I have seen cards on which half-a-dozen "Real Roman Cameos" were mounted exhibited in shop windows, and the price asked was 2s. 6d. each. These scandalous imitations of lovely ornaments will

only be superseded when English workers send
into the market the genuine articles.

Cameo-Cutting Highly Recommended.

The question of the pursuit of Cameo-cutting
as an industrial occupation for ladies was pro-
bably first suggested by Mrs. Henry Mackarness,
the well-known authoress of "A Trap to Catch a
Sunbeam," who strongly recommended the art of
Cameo-cutting in shell to the notice of ladies.
In an admirable work entitled "The Young
Lady's Book," published in 1876, she thus speaks
of the work :—

"It is sufficiently simple to be within the
scope* of many who possess taste, patience, and
deft fingers. . . . It cannot be acquired without some instruction, and considerable perseverance; but the instruction is within reach, and
the perseverance will be amply repaid by the
results." This Cameo-cutting will "give young
ladies a new and elegant pursuit." It will "raise
their thoughts from knitting and netting, and
cultivate a taste for higher pursuits. . . . It
can be practised with half-a-dozen small tools
that take up scarcely any room ; and, with a little
care and instruction, the art can be readily
acquired. Some knowledge of figure-drawing is
necessary, and a correct eye ; and it is needless to
say that the more skilful the artist in this respect,

the better her Cameo-work is likely to be." The *Queen* was the first paper to devote a special illustrated supplement to the question.

The *Lady*, the *Jewish World*, the *Housewife*, the *Manchester Courier*, and other papers as widely separated in their pursuits and politics, have urged the consideration of this work upon public attention.

"In the *Society of Arts Journal*, eighteen months ago"—we quote from the *Jewish World*— "a paper read by Mr. Marsh before that Society was published at length, and copied into journals far and near. Almost at once the work was tried by ladies who had a knowledge of modelling and of wood-carving, and the results obtained furnish the highest possible expectation that in the near future this fascinating art will find a home amongst the ladies of England. There is no machinery required; no dust or dirt is created; there is no risk of soiling dress or carpet; and it is not at all trying to the sight; while the prospects of remuneration are of the brightest possible character. There are an enormous number of Cameos worn as pins, brooches, ear-rings, finger-rings; and the uses to which the Cameo could be put are infinite—as, for instance, for buttons, or for insetting into book-covers, or for wall ornaments. The old fashion was to wear vulgarly large brooches, with heads of abnormal size, so as to show as much ornamentation as possible; but

the new fashion is to make them small, and to cut
modern figures, rejecting those classic heads as-
sociated at times with most questionable stories.
Why ever should ladies run after the face of
Venus or Juno? Is there not as much beauty
and infinitely more poetry to be got out of the
faces of Rebekah or Ruth? Why should men
wear Jupiter or Apollo in preference to Moses
or David? Surely all that art can ever impart
would fail to exhaust the tenderness or the gran-
deur that could be embodied in one of these faces."

Mrs. Macfarlane, writing in the *Housewife*,
September 1888, said:—"It is now suggested
that the industry be taken up in England, as a
remunerative employment for women whose artistic knowledge already embraces some idea of
drawing and modelling, and who do not feel in-
clined to enter the ranks of those who paint well
or indifferently, those little knicknackeries which
it is felt have almost had their day, at least as
far as substantial commercial value is concerned.
Cameo-cutting, in this country, bears the charm
of novelty, is easy to learn, is adaptable to many
uses, and in no way encroaches upon existing
national labour. Cameos representing scenes
from the classics have before now been introduced
into cabinets or boxes, to beautify and make them
more valuable; they may, moreover, be used in
embellishing books and albums. One exquisitely
carved Cameo was shown to me the other day which

represented the face of Christ, and was to be set in the cover of a devotional book, where I am sure it would look most beautiful. Then Cameos may be set in frames to hold photographs on the table, or be inserted in the backs of chairs, instead of the painted scenes or sprays of flowers which were so fashionable a year or two ago. Ladies' and gentlemen's trinkets and apparel open out a wide field for Cameo-work; brooches, ear-rings, breast-pins, studs, links, and finger-rings, are very commonly carved in Italy, but are often made too large for use. Executed finely on small pieces of shell, they might be rendered more acceptable and pretty. A special idea which has been proposed is, that sets of buttons be made of Cameos for coats, yachting, boating, or other garments. Designers who could hit upon some new idea, and carry it out for themselves, might do a good deal in these and divers other ways connected with dress. Cloak-clasps, umbrella and sunshade knobs, fan-handles, dressing-cases, hand-glasses, brush - backs, glove and handkerchief boxes can be made uncommon and beautiful by its application.

"Another range in which the art would flourish is church decoration, for which Cameos are peculiarly appropriate. There is a purity and, at the same time, a durability about them, which commends their use in this direction. How beautiful, for instance, a frieze of palm-leaves would look upon a reredos, or a carved lily upon a memorial stone, or how appropriately a pulpit might be decorated in Cameo! As I write, ideas for church adornment crowd into my mind, but as I have not yet exhausted the resources of Cameo-cutting in another direction, I must leave my readers to imagine these for themselves."

Derivation of the Word "Cameo."

Much curious interest has been excited with respect to the derivation of the word Cameo, and the fact is curious that in that splendid repertory of all things rare, curious, and of interest, "Notes and Queries," the only references to the Cameo are two in number. One is a question propounded in vol. viii., series iv., page 528, in which a correspondent puts the query, which was never answered, "What is the earliest known example of a shell Cameo?" The second reference occurs in vol. iii., series v., in which the derivation of Cameos is inquired for, and the answer appears in vol. iii., on page 31. Here Mr. F. Chance, Sydenham Hall, after learnedly discussing derivations from the Greek, Italian, Latin, German, and Spanish, winds up by saying with Dundreary, that Cameo is one of those words which "no fellow can make out."

"The meaning of the word Cameo," says a writer in the *Housewife*, "is literally a picture of

one colour.   In an ancient dictionary of arts and
sciences, more than a hundred years old, which
I have before me, the word is thus spelt and
explained :—' Camaieu or Camehuia, in Natural
History, the same with camæa.'   I look up
' camæa,' and find the word descanted upon as
follows :—' In Natural History, a genus of the
semi-pellucid gems, approaching to the onyx
structure, being composed of zones, and formed on
a crystalline basis; but having their zones very
broad and thick, and laid alternately on one
another, with no common matter between;
usually less transparent and more debased with
earth than the onyxes.'   Species are then de-
scribed which I need not detail.   Returning next
to the camaieu, I find :—' This word is also used
to express a stone, on which are found various
figures and representations of " landskips," &c.,
formed by a kind of *lusus naturæ,* so as to
exhibit pictures without painting.   It is likewise
applied to any kind of gem on which figures are
engraven, either indentedly or in relievo.' "

The *Queen* newspaper referred also to the
derivation of the term, and added the following
bit of historical research :—

" The term Cameo, in the language of art, is
usually applied to gems or stones that are worked
in relievo, that is, in which the object represented
is raised above the plane of the ground, in con-
tradistinction to intaglio, in which the subject is

engraved or indented. The art of ornamenting precious stones with heads and figures is of high antiquity, but it was for the most part confined to intaglio or indenting, an easier process than relieving the work from a ground. Such stones were used for signets or seals in very remote ages by the Etruscans and the Greeks. One of the first names of great note that occurs in this branch of art is that of Pyrgoteles, who lived in the time of Alexander the Great, and who alone was permitted to engrave seal rings for the King. Tryphon, who lived under the immediate successors of Alexander, also deserves mention here, being the author of a beautiful and well-known Cameo in the Marlborough collection, representing the marriage of Cupid and Psyche.

" In ancient Rome the age of Augustus was re-markable for the excellence of the gem-engravers who were then living, amongst them Dioscorides, some of whose beautiful works have reached our times. Engravers in gems, both in cameo and intaglio, continued to flourish down to Marcus Aurelius. With the decline of the Roman Empire, gem-engraving was neglected, like the other arts, and it was not till the fifteenth century that the taste and munificence of the Medici caused a revival in Italy, and tempted artists to devote themsélves to its practice. Cameos at that time were in great request for personal ornaments, and for inlaying or embossing vases and similar articles.   Cameo collecting became a passion in Italy, and the gem-engravers of that period found special historians in Vasari and Marietti.   In the succeeding century there was a considerable falling off, but in the eighteenth century the art again rose, and the names of some who exercised it will bear comparison with those of almost any age.   The greater part of these were Italians; but two of the most celebrated, John Pichler and Laurence Natter, were natives of Germany, and their works challenge competition with the finest antiques.   In England it was Josiah Wedgwood who revived the taste for Cameo-work by his admirable reproduction of the Barberini Vase, his unsurpassed portrait medallions, and his classical bas-reliefs on plaques, vases, and tea-sets, placed in beautifully tinted jasper, basalt, and other bodies.   James Tassie of Glasgow, by his paste imitations of antique gems, 15,000 in number, also contributed to the popularity of Cameo-work; while W. Brown and Nathanael Marchand were famous as gem-engravers at the beginning of the present century.   Marchand died in 1812 as a member of the Royal Academy, and principal gem-engraver to the King.   The practice of working Cameo on shells is of comparatively modern introduction in Italy, and is carried on particularly in Rome."

A Teacher at Work.

A very widespread interest arose in consequence of the article published in the Journal of the Society of Arts; correspondents in all parts of the United Kingdom wrote asking questions, and several came from far-distant parts to take a lesson. In the neighbourhood of London, heads of technical colleges took up the question in a practical form, and at several teaching is now imparted to such pupils as exhibit an aptitude for drawing and modelling. The results already achieved are highly satisfactory, and the work done by pupils has been publicly exhibited on several occasions. A few practical lessons are, of course, of greater value than learning by correspondence or from a book; yet, notwithstanding the difficulty of beginning to cut without a teacher, many are now producing admirable work, though they have had no other instruction than that contained in the Journal of the Society of Arts.

At first, and for a long time after my paper was read at the Society of Arts, I was placed in a great difficulty by correspondents writing for tools, for shells, and for a teacher. Special tools are now manufactured by Mr. Buck, and a teacher was at length strongly recommended by Mr. John Ford, himself an accomplished Cameo engraver, of the firm of Ford & Wright, diamond polishers, Clerkenwell Green. The gentleman in question was Signor Giovanni,[1] now of London, who obtained great celebrity in Naples and Rome as an engraver of Cameos, and who, while still at the head of his profession, has laboured to restore the almost lost art of engraving on glass. After the work of six years, he completed the ornamentation of a drinking-cup of pure flint crystal, the subject being the training of young Bacchus. For his triumph in this department of art King Humbert I. bestowed upon him the dignity of a Cavaliere of the Crown of Italy. His designs are full of grace and originality; and the future Cameo engravers of England will be greatly indebted to him for the skill with which he has facilitated their acquiring the art. In the course of interviews with Signor Giovanni, I represented to him how very difficult it was for any to perfect themselves in the work without models, and at my entreaty he was good enough to model, mould, and cast a series of examples in plaster of Paris, with the aid of which, though the teacher may not be near, the chief difficulties a learner has to encounter may be easily overcome. These models embrace the anatomical head and neck, the eye, nose and mouth, and chin; fancy heads, portraits, Cupids, classic heads, plants, flowers, fish, and animals.

---

[1] Signor Giovanni has taught with great success at the High School, Cecile House, Crouch End, London; and the principal, Miss E. Rowland, kindly permits references to her, by those desirous of taking lessons, or obtaining materials for the work.

There are twenty-four in the whole series, and they can be had in sets of six, the dozen, or the whole.

Signor Giovanni's method of teaching is first of all to get his pupils to carve an ornament upon a piece of Lava. Selected pieces may be purchased at 4d. per lb., and they make an admirable medium for learning to carve. Then afterwards a piece of shell is taken and the figure is cut in Cameo.

The only English workman who is at present engaged in the work of Cameo engraving is Mr. William King, who learned the art in his apprenticeship to Messrs. Francati & Santamaria. He is spoken of by the members of that firm as being equal to any Roman workman.

Lessons by Correspondence.

If the distance from London is too great for a pupil to come to town, the "roughed" Cameo can be sent to Signor Giovanni by post. He then makes a mould, and produces a cast; this he corrects and returns, so that the pupil can alter and improve the Cameo without the intervention of a foreign hand.

In order to produce a Mould from which to take casts, first lightly oil the surface of the Cameo, place around a cardboard funnel, which can be held in place by an indiarubber band. The plaster of Paris used must be "extra fine;" that most suitable is called "Scagliola," and may be purchased at any oil-shop at 6d. a bag containing a few lbs. Mix a small quantity with water, and pour upon the face of the Cameo. When dry, paint the Mould with French polish until a gloss appears upon the surface. When the Mould is perfectly dry, apply oil to the surface, then pour in plaster of Paris. As many impressions may be taken in this way as are desired without injury to the Mould.

Is there a Market?

I have been frequently asked, "Can I find a market for my Cameos if I learn to cut them?" No one ever put such a question to the drawing-master or to the music-teacher when beginning lessons. But of this new profession the answer is undoubted. As soon as Cameos may be had of better designs than those in the market, purchasers will be found for them. If there is a doubt in the mind of any one on this point, look at the ornaments worn by those one meets in the course of a brief walk through the principal streets of London. I venture to say that difficulty would be found in counting the ear-rings, brooches, pins, and bracelets of Cameo which one sees; nor would any one, if trained in art, approve, in the majority of instances, of the size or design of the Cameos worn.

The taste was formerly to get the largest possible piece of shell, and cut a head about three times the normal size, in order to provide for the greatest amount of ornamentation, with ears of corn or bunches of grapes. A Greek face was often conjoined with Roman or Egyptian ornaments. What, to modern England, is the story of Venus or Cupid, or the beauty of Cleopatra? Are there not a thousand stories in the history of our own land of reputable queens more worthy of illustration? Are the faces of our poets, dramatists, and men of science, letters, and art of less account than the faces of Apollo, Bacchus, or Pericles? Putting aside the historical gallery, are there not amongst the circle of our relatives and friends, faces dear beyond all comparison with those of Hebe or of Neptune?

Take another field of labour, that of flowers. We have all studied their language, and know what is meant by the gift of a rose, a lily, or a forget-me-not. But the flower fades all too quickly for the expression of the feeling which love conveys; how much more beautiful, then, is the gift of a flower wrought by the hand of a loved one—a flower that will never fade!

Fashion is ever introducing new adaptations of ornament to dress. Note the two or three buttons with which a lady's loose jacket is now fastened on the left. Why not carve these in Cameo, a dainty design in white on a purple or red or brown background, glowing like a precious stone? These would look beautiful!

The uses to which the Cameo may be put are innumerable, and in what I have said I have confined myself to those of personal adornment only, leaving out altogether the hundred and one purposes of ornamentation about the house, the table, or the drawing-room.

Designs.

The following pages contain a miscellaneous collection of designs suitable for a great variety of uses, more suggestive than exhaustive in their character and scope. They will be found useful for practice, but the artist will soon find subjects better adapted to the degree of skill attained. A large number are from the plaster casts modelled by Signor Giovanni.